The Quotation Bank

Dr Jekyll and Mr Hyde

Robert Louis Stevenson

Copyright © 2019 Esse Publishing Limited

First published in 2016 by:
The Quotation Bank
Esse Publishing Limited

10 9 8 7 6 5

A CIP catalogue record for this book is available from the British Library.
ISBN 978-0-9956086-4-1

All enquiries to: contact@thequotationbank.co.uk

Printed and bound by Target Print Limited, Broad Lane, Cottenham, Cambridge CB24 8SW.

www.thequotationbank.co.uk

Introduction

What examiners are looking for   4

How The Quotation Bank can help you in your exams   5

How to use The Quotation Bank   6

Quotations

Story of the Door *to* Incident at the Window   7

The Last Night   15

Dr Lanyon's Narrative   17

Henry Jekyll's Full Statement of the Case   21

Revision and Essay Planning

Major Themes and Characters   32

How to revise effectively   33

Sample essay, potential essay questions and revision activities   34

Glossary   41

Welcome to The Quotation Bank, the comprehensive guide to all the key quotations you need to succeed in your exams.

Whilst you may have read the novel, watched a film adaptation, understood the plot and have a strong grasp of context, the vast majority of marks awarded in your GCSE are for the ability to write a focused essay, full of quotations, and most importantly, quotations that you then analyse.

I think we all agree it is **analysis** that is the tricky part – and that is why we are here to help!

The Quotation Bank takes 25 of the most important quotations from the text, interprets them, analyses them, highlights literary techniques Stevenson has used, puts them in context, and suggests which quotations you might use in which essays.

At the end of **The Quotation Bank** we have put together a sample answer, essay plans and great revision exercises to help you prepare for your exam. We have also included a detailed glossary to make sure you completely understand what certain literary terms actually mean!

English Literature 9-1: What are examiners looking for?

All GCSE Exam Boards mark your exams using the same Assessment Objectives (AOs) – around 80% of your mark across the English Literature GCSE will be awarded for A01 and A02.

A01	Read, understand and respond to texts. Students should be able to: • Maintain a critical style and develop an *informed personal response* • Use textual references, *including quotations*, to support and illustrate *interpretations*.
A02	Analyse the *Language, Form and Structure* used by a writer to *create meanings and effects*, using *relevant subject terminology* where appropriate.

Basically, **AO1** is the ability to answer the question set, showing a good knowledge of the text, and using quotations to back up ideas and interpretations.

AO2 is the ability to analyse these quotations, as well as the literary techniques the writer uses, and to show you understand the effect of these on the reader.

We will also highlight elements of **AO3** – the context in which the novel is set.

How The Quotation Bank can help you in your exams.

The Quotation Bank is designed to make sure that every point you make in an essay clearly fulfils the Assessment Objectives an examiner will be using when marking your work.

Every quotation comes with the following detailed material:

Interpretation: The interpretation of each quotation allows you to fulfil **AO1**, responding to the text and giving an informed personal response.

Techniques: Using subject-specific terminology correctly (in this case, the literary devices used by Stevenson) is a key part of **AO2**.

Analysis: We have provided as much analysis (**AO2**) as possible. It is a great idea to analyse the quotation in detail – you need to do more than just say what it means, but also what effect the language, form and structure has on the reader.

Use in essays on… Your answer needs to be focused to fulfil **AO1**. This section helps you choose relevant quotations and link them together for a stronger essay.

How to use The Quotation Bank.

Many students spend time learning quotations by heart.

This is an excellent idea, but they often forget what they are meant to do with those quotations once they get into the exam!

By using **The Quotation Bank**, not only will you have a huge number of quotations to use in your essays, you will also have ideas on what to say about them, how to analyse them, how to link them together, and what questions to use them for.

For GCSE essay questions, these quotations can form the basis of your answer, making sure every point comes **directly from the text (AO1)** and allowing you to **analyse language, form and structure (AO2)**. We also highlight where you can easily and effectively include **context (AO3)**.

For GCSE questions that give you an extract to analyse, the quotations in **The Quotation Bank** are excellent not only for revising the skills of **analysis (AO2)**, but also for showing **wider understanding of the text (AO1)**.

Story of the Door:
"**Cold, scanty and embarrassed in discourse; backward in sentiment; lean, long, dusty, dreary, and yet somehow lovable.**"

Interpretation: This description of Utterson introduces a stereotypical 19th Century British gentleman – private and unemotional with a reserved personality.

Techniques: Alliteration; Language; Adjectives.

Analysis:

- The alliteration of the "l" and "d" sounds are deep and heavy, mimicking the dull, tedious personality of Utterson.
- The adjectives used to describe Utterson emphasise the sort of life Jekyll later rejects – they have associations with a boring, lacklustre lifestyle where the current way of life is never questioned.
- "Cold" and "embarrassed in discourse" highlight the value placed on privacy – it is this cloak of secrecy that allows Jekyll to experiment uninterrupted.

Use in essays on…Secrecy; Repression; Utterson; Society.

Story of the Door:
  "The man trampled calmly over the child's body and left her screaming on the ground…it wasn't like a man; it was like some damned Juggernaut."

Interpretation: We have the first depiction of Hyde's evil nature, and Stevenson deliberately inflicts it on a child to increase the reader's fear of Hyde's character.

Techniques: Juxtaposition; Imagery; Oxymoron.

Analysis:
- The contrasting "man" against "child" is threatening, but the oxymoronic "trampled calmly" shows Hyde is naturally comfortable with violence.
- Referencing the "child's body" dehumanises the victim, and the image of her "screaming" is a powerful sensual depiction of Hyde's cruelty.
- "Damned" refers to Hyde's sinful nature, with the image of "Juggernaut" suggesting a violent, powerful force surging forwards in an unstoppable manner.

Use in essays on…Good and evil; Religion; Violence; Innocence.

Search for Mr Hyde:

"...A volume of some dry divinity on his reading-desk, until the clock of the neighbouring church rang out the hour of twelve, when he would go soberly and gratefully to bed."

Interpretation: Utterson contrasts with Jekyll, as he rigidly sticks to structure, order and rationality, maintaining a routine and socially acceptable lifestyle.

Techniques: Adverbs; Language; Alliteration.

Analysis:

- The heavy, dull alliteration of "d" in "dry divinity" refers to religious restrictions and lack of vibrancy that typifies Christianity in the 19th Century.
- Utterson's reading material is a "volume", suggesting many more volumes offering rules and restrictions as to how one should live.
- The church dictates when Utterson sleeps, which is without enthusiasm for a new day ("soberly"), and he is relieved the day is over ("gratefully").

Use in essays on…Religion; Desire and repression; Utterson.

Dr Jekyll was quite at Ease:
"The large handsome face of Dr Jekyll grew pale to the very lips, and there
came a blackness about his eyes."

Interpretation: Jekyll's cheerful and pleasant demeanour rapidly disappears when he is questioned about his will – the change from good to evil is disturbingly quick.

Techniques: Juxtaposition; Colour; Language.

Analysis:

- The juxtaposition of Jekyll's "handsome" face with his pale lips and black eyes shows that man's dual nature is not just a mental conflict, but also a physical one.
- "Pale" has associations with the death that comes later in the novel. The "blackness" of "his eyes" alludes to the darkness of Hyde's soul.
- Since Jekyll's lips "grew" pale, and blackness "came…about" his eyes, the reader gets a sense of evil spreading over him uncontrollably.

Use in essays on…Duality of Man; Good and evil; Jekyll.

The Carew Murder Case:
"And next moment, with ape-like fury, he was trampling his victim under foot, and hailing down a storm of blows, under which the bones were audibly shattered and the body jumped upon the roadway."

Interpretation: Brutal, animalistic violence and evil fill this image – the almost inhuman destruction of another human life highlights the power of evil.

Techniques: Simile; Language; Metaphor.

Analysis:
- The simile "ape-like" gives Hyde strong animal characteristics but also suggests he has not yet evolved from animals, and as he inflicts a metaphorical "storm of blows" he is also seen as a brutal force of nature.
- Hyde's victim becomes totally dehumanised – he is nothing more than "his victim", "bones" and a "body" rather than a person, and is "shattered".
- The swiftness of these actions is frightening – it all occurs in a "moment".

Use in essays on…Violence; Good and evil; Innocence.

Incident of the Letter:

"A yard which had once been a garden, to the building which was indifferently known as the laboratory or the dissecting-rooms…and his own tastes being rather chemical than anatomical…"

Interpretation: Jekyll inhabits a highly scientific environment, rejecting the simple pleasures of the old garden – he prefers the appeal of chemistry to the natural world.

Techniques: Setting; Language; Adverb.

Analysis:

- This was once a "garden", a natural, wholesome place of relaxation, but has been replaced by the scientific experimentation of "the laboratory".
- Science was a threat to religion in the 19th Century as it often contradicted religious teachings. Jekyll's "tastes being rather chemical" refers to the fact that he desires scientific exploration over Utterson's "dry divinity".
- The adverb "indifferently" reinforces ideas of privacy and secrecy – Jekyll commits horrific acts as people are "indifferent" to his actions.

Use in essays on…Science; Religion; Secrecy.

Remarkable Incident of Dr Lanyon:
"He had his death-warrant written legibly upon his face. The rosy man had grown pale; his flesh had fallen away."

Interpretation: The reader is graphically shown the transformation of Lanyon and the physical deterioration of his person when he discovers Jekyll's secret.

Techniques: Juxtaposition; Alliteration.

Analysis:
- "Rosy man" has associations with vibrant colour and a natural, healthy lifestyle, which juxtaposes "pale" and its deathly connotations.
- The alliteration of the fluid "f" sound underlines the fact that Lanyon's flesh is literally slipping from his bones, much like when Jekyll turns into Hyde.
- A "death-warrant" is an official document ordering an execution. Whilst "death-warrant" foreshadows the deaths of Lanyon and Jekyll, it also reminds us of the sins committed and the justice that must come.

Use in essays on…Duality of Man; Good and evil; Lanyon.

Incident at the Window:

"The smile was struck out of his face and succeeded by an expression of such abject terror and despair, as froze the very blood of the two gentlemen."

Interpretation: Jekyll no longer controls Hyde's appearances, and Jekyll's sudden transformation causes extreme physical reactions from Utterson and Enfield.

Techniques: Sibilance; Language.

Analysis:

- The sibilance in "smile was struck" quickens the pace with which the pleasant "smile" is replaced by "abject terror and despair".
- "Smile" is a gentle image, and is removed forcefully and violently when it is "struck out". Hyde causes a physical reaction in all he meets, and "froze the very blood" of two men we know to be sensible, rational gentlemen.
- "Succeeded" has associations with victory – there is a clear sense of a battle between good and evil, and here evil is victorious.

Use in essays on…Good and evil; The Supernatural; Violence.

The Last Night:

"When that masked thing like a monkey jumped from among the chemicals and whipped into the cabinet, it went down my spine like ice…I give you my bible-word it was Mr Hyde!"

Interpretation: Science and religion clash in a destructive manner – Hyde is animalistic, surrounded by science, and Poole turns to religion to make sense of it.

Techniques: Simile; Imagery; Language; Setting.

Analysis:

- Hyde is a non-human "thing" and is "masked", hidden from society. Fear would be increased for 19th Century readers – he is "among the chemicals", dangerous scientific experimentation that could challenge religion.
- The simile "like a monkey" reinforces Hyde's animalistic nature and again he has a physical effect on other people ("down my spine like ice").
- Religion is needed to try to make sense of this; Poole gives his "bible-word".

Use in essays on…Religion; Science; The Supernatural; Secrecy.

The Last Night:
  "One lay beside the tea things open, and Utterson was amazed to find it a copy of a pious work for which Jekyll had several times expressed a great esteem, annotated, in his own hand, with startling blasphemies."

Interpretation: Jekyll is often seen as a character who embraces science, which is dangerous enough – here we see an explicit, blasphemous rejection of religion.

Techniques: Symbolism; Language; Juxtaposition.

Analysis:

- The "tea things" are a traditional symbol of British manners – taken at a set time, it is a calm, gentlemanly occasion of respectability.
- Utterson has "great esteem" for strict, rigid religion – "Pious" links to "dry divinity". Jekyll rebels against rigidity in religion, shown in Hyde's scribbles.
- The dual nature of man is evident in the juxtaposition of "pious" with the "blasphemies" in the book – Hyde startlingly rejects religious teachings.

Use in essays on…Religion; Science; Good and evil.

Dr Lanyon's Narrative:

"The phial…might have been about half full of a blood-red liquor, which was highly pungent to the sense of smell, and seemed to me to contain phosphorous and some volatile ether."

Interpretation: Lanyon's description of what he finds in Jekyll's private cabinet is disturbing – Lanyon cannot make sense of it, and it is depicted as clearly dangerous.

Techniques: Sensual language; Adjectives.

Analysis:

- Fear of science stemmed from its unknown qualities. "A", "seemed" and "some" show even Dr Lanyon cannot make sense of Jekyll's experiments.
- Jekyll's scientific exploration links to violence. "Blood-red" alludes to Hyde's bloodshed, and "volatile" mimics the unstable nature of Jekyll and Hyde.
- "Highly pungent" shows Jekyll offending the senses as well as our morals. His behaviour is literally and metaphorically rotten.

Use in essays on…Science; Violence; Secrecy.

Dr Lanyon's Narrative:
"There was something abnormal and misbegotten in the very essence of the creature that now faced me – something seizing, surprising and revolting."

Interpretation: Lanyon struggles to articulate exactly what Hyde is – even standing in front of him, the description is clearly not human.

Techniques: Sibilance; Tri-colon (or list of three); Imagery; Repetition.

Analysis:
- The sibilance in "something seizing, surprising" is a traditionally gothic sound, creating a sinister tone of fear, terror and menace.
- Hyde's effect on Lanyon is all-consuming – it controls his body ("seizing"), shocks his mind ("surprising") and disgusts his morals ("revolting").
- Hyde is impossible to define – Lanyon calls him a "creature", giving him animal characteristics, but the repetition of "something" demonstrates that Dr Lanyon cannot identify what it is about Hyde that makes him so hideous.

Use in essays on…Good and evil; The Supernatural.

Dr Lanyon's Narrative:
"A new province of knowledge and new avenues to fame and power shall be laid open to you, here, in this room, upon the instant; and your sight shall be blasted by a prodigy to stagger the unbelief of Satan."

Interpretation: Having helped a friend, Lanyon is offered a chance to leave Hyde or to observe something staggering and evil. Lanyon, usually so rational, chooses evil.

Techniques: Religious allusions; Repetition; Irony.

Analysis:
- The repetition of "new" is threatening. It will "open to you" unknown consequences, and with "fame and power" as a motive, it is clearly unethical.
- The speed evil consumes good is clear – it will happen "upon the instant".
- Scientific exploration is as equally devastating as original sin. "New province of knowledge" alludes to the devil tempting Eve, yet Hyde's evil will "stagger the unbelief of Satan", depicting him as worse than the devil.

Use in essays on…Science; Religion; Desire and repression.

Dr Lanyon's Narrative:
    " 'O God!' I screamed, and 'O God!' again and again."

Interpretation: The level of disbelief in the supernatural events before him, and the evil he is witnessing, leads Lanyon to desperately call out to God to protect him.

Techniques: Repetition; Language.

Analysis:

- Lanyon, Utterson and Enfield are known throughout the novel as rational, coherent and eloquent. Lanyon's repetitive cry of "O God!" is both an uncontrolled scream of horror but also a direct plea to God to protect him.
- It is important to remember that Lanyon is desperately seeking support from God and religion in the face of supreme evil, and that God cannot provide it, as Lanyon dies from the horror of what he sees. Essentially, evil defeats religion.

Use in essays on…Religion; Good and evil; The Supernatural.

Henry Jekyll's Full Statement of the Case:
"My imperious desire to carry my head high, and wear a more than commonly grave countenance before the public. Hence it came about that I concealed my pleasures."

Interpretation: Jekyll explains that he has a desperate desire to be socially acceptable and behave in the sombre way society expects, hence he represses his own desires.

Techniques: Language; Alliteration.

Analysis:
- The alliteration of "head high" stresses the fact that society demands people maintain their reputation and dignity. For Jekyll this is stifling.
- The idea that Jekyll would "wear" a socially respectable persona has associations with a costume. He is acting a part as Jekyll, and his true character is actually Hyde – this is where his "pleasures" lie.
- "Concealed" has associations of being hidden away, straining to break free.

Use in essays on…Duality of man; Good and evil; Desire and repression.

Henry Jekyll's Full Statement of the Case:
"I was no more myself when I laid aside restraint and plunged in shame, than when I laboured, in the eye of day, at the furtherance of knowledge or the relief of sorrow and suffering."

Interpretation: Jekyll is explicit – he was equally himself when he was submitting to his desires and committing dreadful acts as he was when he was engaging in good.

Techniques: Juxtaposition; Alliteration.

Analysis:

- Alliteration in "no more myself" stresses the word "myself" – Jekyll's self is dual and features both "shame" and "knowledge".
- "Laid aside" and "plunged" are active, dynamic descriptions – Jekyll vigorously pursues "shame", yet doing good is "laboured" and tiresome.
- Good takes place in "the eye of day" – evil is for night. Evil brings "shame", but sibilance stresses good can bring "the relief of sorrow and suffering".

Use in essays on…Duality of man; Good and evil; Desire and repression.

Henry Jekyll's Full Statement of the Case:
"I thus drew steadily nearer to that truth by whose partial discovery I have been doomed to such a dreadful shipwreck: that man is not truly one, but truly two."

Interpretation: Jekyll is convinced that man has a dual nature, that we are both good and evil – however, he acknowledges that this realisation is a dangerous one.

Techniques: Repetition; Imagery.

Analysis:

- Jekyll's conclusion is correct – "steadily", "truth" and "discovery" convey rational analysis and show his conclusions are accurate, not blasphemous.
- The repetition of "truly" links to "truth" earlier in the statement – Jekyll is indeed correct, and should not be judged for his discovery; it is simple truth.
- Jekyll's conclusion is "a dreadful shipwreck", with associations of fear and danger, and he is "doomed", which suggests religious judgement from God.

Use in essays on…Duality of man; Good and evil; Science; Religion.

Henry Jekyll's Full Statement of the Case:
"Before the course of my scientific discoveries had begun to suggest the most naked possibility of such a miracle, I had learned to dwell with pleasure, as a beloved daydream, on the thought of the separation of these elements."

Interpretation: Whilst Jekyll becomes a slave to Hyde, he began his "course" with the intention of simply separating the two sides of man, not the pursuit of evil.

Techniques: Imagery; Language.

Analysis:
- Jekyll discovers Hyde, not creates him. "Scientific discoveries", "possibility" and "suggest" show Hyde already existed – Jekyll simply uncovers him.
- Jekyll's intentions were pure. The image of a "beloved daydream", "miracle" and "pleasure" allude to wholesome motives, not the pursuit of horror.
- The description of man's dual nature as "elements" has scientific associations – Jekyll's motivations were scientific, not anti-religious.

Use in essays on…Desire and repression; Science; Religion; Innocence.

Henry Jekyll's Full Statement of the Case:
"The trembling immateriality, the mist-like transience, of this seemingly so
solid body in which we walk attired."

Interpretation: Jekyll considers a further aspect of the dual nature of man. Whilst humans may seem strong, we are in fact insignificant and temporary in this world.

Techniques: Sibilance; Imagery; Language.

Analysis:

- The sibilance of "seemingly so solid" stresses the irony of the human condition. We are anything but solid, but don't wish to accept this truth.
- The image of humans being "attired" has dramatic associations. We wear costumes to hide vulnerabilities, and our "walk" is simply a performance.
- Jekyll embraces human frailty. The image of "trembling immateriality" highlights physical insignificance, and "mist-like transience" emphasises our fleeting impact on the world. Jekyll's aim is to explore these ideas.

Use in essays on…Religion; Science; Duality of man.

Henry Jekyll's Full Statement of the Case:
"The most racking pangs succeeded: a grinding in the bones, deadly nausea, and a horror of the spirit that cannot be exceeded at the hour of birth or death."

Interpretation: Jekyll's description of his transformation to Hyde is both gruesomely painful, but also alludes to something disturbingly natural and powerful.

Techniques: Language; Allusions; Imagery.

Analysis:

- The physical agony ("racking pangs" and "grinding") makes clear Hyde is the unnatural state, yet allusions to "death", "birth" and the associated "nausea" could suggest that Hyde and evil are part of the human life cycle.
- Turning into Hyde is not just physically destructive – he also destroys the "spirit" with his "horror".
- "Succeeded" is a subtle use of language – evil is associated with victory.

Use in essays on…Good and evil; Duality of man; Violence.

Henry Jekyll's Full Statement of the Case:
"I knew myself, at the first breath of this new life, to be more wicked, tenfold
more wicked, sold a slave to my original evil; and the thought, in that
moment, braced and delighted me like wine."

Interpretation: Jekyll's first transformation to Hyde confirms instantly that Hyde is
evil – however, the reader is disturbed to see Jekyll's confession that it was a delight.

Techniques: Simile; Sibilance; Allusions; Repetition.

Analysis:

- Repetition of "wicked" and "tenfold" leaves no doubt as to Hyde's evil
  nature, and "delighted me like wine" refers to evil's intoxicating effect.
- "Sold a slave" stresses the word "slave", suggesting evil entraps Jekyll,
  reinforced by the use of "braced".
- "My original evil" again references Eve's original sin, suggesting sin is a
  natural part of man, but "new life" has a tone of excitement and potential.

Use in essays on…Duality of man; Good and evil; Religion; Desire and repression.

Henry Jekyll's Full Statement of the Case:
"The drug had no discriminating action; it was neither diabolical nor divine;
it but shook the doors of the prison-house of my disposition."

Interpretation: It is not the drug that created Hyde – Jekyll makes clear that the drug simply releases whatever is inside man, and in this case, that was Edward Hyde.

Techniques: Metaphor; Alliteration.

Analysis:
- The alliteration of "diabolical nor divine" supports the idea that nothing is purely "diabolical" (meaning of the devil) or purely "divine" (meaning of God) – most things are a combination of both.
- 19th Century society, and the way it forced people to conform, is a "prison-house" – it is nothing more than a jail in which people are repressed.
- The events of the novel are not the fault of science – the drug was not the cause of the horror, it simply "shook" the natural behaviours inside Jekyll.

Use in essays on…Desire and repression; Science; Religion; Duality of man.

Henry Jekyll's Full Statement of the Case:
"I was the first that could thus plod in the public eye with a load of genial respectability, and in a moment, like a schoolboy, strip off these lendings and spring headlong into the sea of liberty."

Interpretation: The socially acceptable way to behave is tedious and restrictive – Jekyll sees his discovery as a way of unburdening himself and becoming free.

Techniques: Simile; Metaphor; Alliteration; Juxtaposition.

Analysis:
- The dull "p" sound and link to "plod" shows the heavy, tiresome manner in which one had to behave, juxtaposed with a dynamic freedom in "spring".
- "Like a schoolboy" conjures images of youth, excitement and vitality, and a sense of freedom unburdened by adult conventions.
- The removal of "lendings" means Jekyll is no longer acting a part, with the scale of freedom when embracing desires emphasised by a "sea of liberty".

Use in essays on…Duality of man; Good and evil; Desire and repression.

Henry Jekyll's Full Statement of the Case:
 "His every act and thought centred on self; drinking pleasure with bestial avidity from any degree of torture to another; relentless like a man of stone."

Interpretation: Hyde's wickedness extends beyond simply harming others – he is selfish, takes joy in the suffering of others, and displays no compassion for humanity.

Techniques: Simile; Sentence structure; Language.

Analysis:

- "Every act and thought" affirms Hyde is entirely evil in both body and soul.
- "Drinking", "pleasure" and "avidity" (greed) have associations with wild over-indulgence, linked with the animal, "bestial" nature of his conduct.
- "Man of stone" suggests Hyde is hard, unmoving and soulless – the use of semi-colons to create a list of his faults, alongside his "relentless" pursuit of "torture", creates a truly terrifying depiction.

Use in essays on…Good and evil; Desire and repression; Violence.

Henry Jekyll's Full Statement of the Case:
"He, I say – I cannot say, I. That child of Hell had nothing human; nothing lived in him but fear and hatred."

Interpretation: Despite Jekyll's understanding that Hyde is a dual part of him, he still cannot bring himself to say "I" as Hyde is too evil to be considered human.

Techniques: 3rd Person; Imagery.

Analysis:

- "That child of Hell" continues Hyde's association with the devil and diabolical behaviour – calling him a child suggests he has grown and been nurtured under the guidance of Hell itself.
- The use of the 3rd person ("he" rather than "I") is Jekyll's refusal to accept that Hyde is a human part of him – despite his acknowledgement that man is "truly two", Hyde is still considered inhuman.
- Hyde's Gothic, supernatural elements are explicit – he is not of this world.

Use in essays on…Religion; Supernatural; Violence; Good and evil.

Major Themes

Duality of Man	Good and Evil	The Supernatural
Repression	Innocence	Science
Violence	Secrecy	Reason
Religion	Society	Desire

Major Characters

Dr Henry Jekyll	Gabriel John Utterson	Mr Edward Hyde
Dr Hastie Lanyon	Richard Enfield	Sir Danvers Carew
	Poole	

How to revise effectively.

One mistake people often make is to try to revise EVERYTHING!

This is clearly not possible.

Instead, once you know and understand the plot, a great idea is to pick three or four major themes, and three or four major characters, and revise these in great detail.

If, for example, you revised Utterson and Lanyon, you will also have covered a huge amount of material to use in questions about Science, Religion or Secrecy.

Or, if you revised Violence and Good and Evil, you would certainly have plenty of material if a question on Jekyll, the Duality of Man or Desire was set.

Use the following framework as a basis for setting **any** of your own revision questions – simply swap the theme or character to create a new essay title!

How does Stevenson portray the theme of _____ in *Dr Jekyll and Mr Hyde*?

How does the character of _____ develop as the novel progresses?

A sample essay paragraph (top level), using ideas directly from
The Quotation Bank (page 8).

How does Stevenson's depiction of violence create a sense of fear?

One depiction of violence that creates a real sense of fear is Stevenson's use of it as a defining characteristic of Edward Hyde; however, it is not simply the violent pain he inflicts that causes a sense of fear in both the reader and those around him, but rather who he inflicts it on, how quickly he engages in violence, and the pleasure with which he does it. The reader's first depiction of Hyde's evil nature is a violent incident, and Stevenson deliberately has Hyde inflict it on a child to increase the reader's fear of his character. In Enfield's telling of the incident, <u>"the man trampled calmly over the child's body and left her screaming on the ground…it wasn't like a man; it was like some damned Juggernaut"</u>. The contrasting depiction of a <u>"man"</u> violently clashing with a <u>"child"</u> is threatening enough and creates a great sense of fear of Hyde, but the oxymoronic <u>"trampled calmly"</u> shows Hyde is naturally comfortable with violence in a society that fears it. Furthermore, referencing the <u>"child's body"</u> dehumanises the victim, as if Hyde doesn't even see her as a person, let alone an innocent child, and the image of her <u>"screaming"</u> is a powerful sensual depiction of Hyde's cruelty and violence, creating fear in the reader.

Potential Essay Questions

How does Stevenson depict religion in the novel?

Topic Sentence 1: Religion is portrayed as providing clear guidance and instruction as to how one should live their life.

Use: Pages 9 and 16.

Topic Sentence 2: Furthermore, characters turn to religion for safety in times of fear and danger.

Use: Pages 15 and 20.

Topic Sentence 3: For Jekyll, religion is stifling and he wishes to break free.

Use: Pages 21, 27 and 28.

Topic Sentence 4: Essentially, religion cannot suppress the evil nature of man.

Use: Pages 19 and 31.

How is the duality of man portrayed in *Dr Jekyll and Mr Hyde*?

Topic Sentence 1: Stevenson makes the dual nature of man explicit through his physical descriptions of characters.

Use: Pages 10, 13 and 14.

Topic Sentence 2: Alongside the physical portrayal, a mental awareness of man's dual nature seems to be portrayed as deeply enticing.

Use: Pages 19 and 24.

Topic Sentence 3: Once the dual nature of one's personality is embraced, it is portrayed as liberating.

Use: Pages 27 and 29.

Topic Sentence 4: Fundamentally, one side of man's nature seems to eventually dominate the other.

Use: Pages 28 and 30.

How does the character of Jekyll develop throughout the novel?

Topic Sentence 1: Jekyll is depicted as a scientific man in a world controlled and restricted by religion.

Use: Pages 12, 17 and 24.

Topic Sentence 2: The pressures of religious conformity clearly influence Jekyll's behaviour.

Use: Pages 21 and 22.

Topic Sentence 3: In reaction to conformity, Jekyll seeks to embrace freedom and knowledge.

Use: Pages 27 and 29.

Topic Sentence 4: As the novel ends, we see the acknowledgement that Jekyll's scientific exploration has discovered evil within man.

Use: Pages 19, 30 and 31.

How is the idea of evil conveyed in *Dr Jekyll and Mr Hyde*?

Topic Sentence 1: Evil takes many forms in the novel, but the most explicit examples are of the violence inflicted upon innocent victims.

Use: Pages 11 and 30.

Topic Sentence 2: This evil is extended beyond violence to a complete disregard for the wellbeing of all humanity.

Use: Pages 8 and 27.

Topic Sentence 3: Furthermore, evil is not always physical, but also takes the form of blasphemy and attacks on religion.

Use: Pages 16, 19 and 31.

Topic Sentence 4: Essentially, evil has the ability to control and influence the body and soul.

Use: Pages 10 and 18.

Suggested Revision Activities

Major character and themes – **Take any of the major characters and themes (see page 32 for a list) and group together quotations in sets of 2 or 3 to answer the following question: "How does the theme/character develop as the novel goes on?"**

You should try to get 4 sets of quotations, giving you 8-12 overall.

A great cover and repeat exercise – **Cover the whole page, apart from the quotation at the top. Can you now fill in the four sections in your exercise book without looking – Interpretations, Techniques, Analysis, Use in essays on…?**

This also works really well as a revision activity with a friend **– cover the whole card, apart from the quotation at the top. If you read out the quotation, can they tell you the four sections without looking – Interpretations, Techniques, Analysis, Use in essays on…?**

"The Development Game" – **Pick any quotation at random from The Quotation Bank and use it to create an essay question, and then create a focused topic sentence to start the essay. Next, find another appropriate quotation to develop your idea even further.**

"The Contrast Game" – **Follow the same rules as The Development Game, but instead of finding a quotation to support your idea, find a quotation that can be used to start a counter-argument.**

Your very own Quotation Bank! **Using the same headings and format as The Quotation Bank, find 10 more quotations from throughout the text (select them from many different sections of the text to help develop whole text knowledge) and create your own revision cards.**

Essay writing – **They aren't always fun, but writing essays is great revision. Choose a practice question and then try taking three quotations and writing out a perfect paragraph, making sure you add connectives, technical vocabulary and sophisticated language.**

Glossary

Alliteration – Repetition of the same consonant or sound at the beginning of a number of words in a sentence: the heavy, dull alliteration of "d" in "dry divinity" alludes to religious restrictions and lack of vibrancy.

Allusions – Referring to something in a sentence without mentioning it explicitly: "a new province of knowledge" alludes to the Tree of Knowledge in the Garden of Eden, therefore linking Hyde's temptation of Lanyon with sin.

Imagery – Figurative language that appeals to the senses of the audience: "trembling immateriality" allows the reader to physically feel the idea of human vulnerability.

Irony – A statement that suggests one thing but often has a contrary meaning: "seemingly so solid" highlights how we believe we are so solid and strong as humans, when in fact Jekyll proves we are the complete opposite.

Juxtaposition – Two ideas, images or words placed next to each other to create a contrasting effect: "handsome" suggests Jekyll's good looks, yet "pale lips" suggests an almost deathly look to him.

Language – The vocabulary chosen to create effect.

Metaphor – A word or phrase used to describe something else so that the first idea takes on the associations of the second: "the prison-house of my disposition" means Jekyll's natural character has been locked away.

Oxymoron – A figure of speech where apparently contradictory terms appear together: "trampled calmly" links violent actions with calm, thoughtful behaviour.

Repetition – When a word, phrase or idea is repeated to reinforce it: Jekyll's description of Hyde's "wicked" nature emphasises the change in his character.

Sentence Structure – The way the writer has ordered the words in a sentence to create a certain effect: the use of semi-colons in the list of Hyde's faults seems to extend the scale of his evil nature.

Setting – The time, place and physical environment of where something takes place: Jekyll's neglect of a garden and focus on the laboratory represents his rejection of the natural order of things and an embracing of the scientific world.

Sibilance – A variation on alliteration, usually of the 's' sound, that creates a hissing sound: "smile was struck" emphasises the speed with which the smile was replaced by fear.

Simile – A comparison of one thing with something of a different kind, used to make a description more vivid: "like a monkey" depicts Hyde as both animalistic but also unevolved.

Symbolism – The use of a symbol to represent an idea: the "tea things" upon Jekyll's table symbolise the traditional, ordered way of behaving in society.

Tri-colon – A list of three words or phrases for effect: "seizing, surprising and revolting" illustrate the complete control Hyde has over all elements of the people he meets.